Everyday German for Comprehension

Ian MacDonald
Head of Modern Languages,
Robert Clack Comprehensive School, Dagenham

Hodder & Stoughton
LONDON SYDNEY AUCKLAND TORONTO

Acknowledgements
The Publishers would like to thank the following for permission to reproduce copyright material: *Bild-Zeitung* (item 46); *Die Welt* (item 48).

British Library Cataloguing in Publication Data

MacDonald, Ian
Everyday German for Comprehension.
1. German language
I. Title
428'.2'421 PF3112

ISBN 0 7131 0323 X

First published 1979
Sixth impression 1991

Printed in Great Britain for the educational publishing division of Hodder and Stoughton Ltd, Mill Road, Dunton Green, Sevenoaks, Kent by Athenaeum Press Ltd, Newcastle upon Tyne.

Contents

To the Teacher

This book comprises a number of items in German for comprehension. The items are graded in difficulty, ranging from simple words and phrases to short newspaper articles.

When working on the exercises, students are not required to express themselves in German. What is being tested is their ability to understand everyday 'authentic' German when they encounter it.

It has long been my wish to see students tackling the kind of German which is seen on notices in Germany; read in newspapers, on menus and in advertisements; heard from loudspeakers at railway stations, on television and radio, and so on. This is, after all, the German that is really relevant to practical requirements in the everyday world, and therefore the German that is much more likely to interest and to motivate.

This type of 'authentic' German is already beginning to appear on the papers set by examination boards and teachers across the country, and it is an area which is rightly developing fast.

Teachers who have not yet worked with material of this nature will be agreeably surprised by the high standards which many pupils can attain. Even pupils who have been unsuccessful in the traditional skills of written production in the foreign language can still achieve a vast amount in the way of comprehension, which is arguably the most valuable skill of all.

Revision tests are incorporated at regular intervals so that students may measure their progress and retention of the vocabulary encountered. There is a Final Test at the end of the book, based on words and phrases chosen from all the exercises.

I.M.

To the Pupil

The words and passages in this book are all examples of 'real' German. In other words, they could all be seen in German newspapers, notices in shops, advertisements and restaurant menus, or heard in announcements at ports and railway stations, or on radio and television.

They are all examples of German which you will see, read and hear in Germany, and yet the exercises are by no means as difficult as you might imagine - simply because everyone who learns a foreign language can *understand* much more than he can *write* or *speak.*

That is the point of the exercises - to try to understand as much as you possibly can. You will probably surprise yourself with just how much you can understand. All your answers will be in English. If you start off with the shorter and simpler exercises at the beginning of the book, it will not be long before you can progress to the longer advertisements and newspaper reports towards the end.

I.M.

1 Weather Forecast (1)

All the words supplied in the left-hand column are frequently used in German weather forecasts. Match each word with its correct meaning chosen from the right-hand column.

1	Sonne	A	Rain
2	Donner	B	Snow
3	Windig	C	Drizzle
4	Nebel	D	Stormy
5	Aufklärung	E	Cold
6	Schnee	F	Fog
7	Sprühregen	G	Thunder
8	Regen	H	Sunshine
9	Stürmisch	I	Brighter weather
10	Kalt	J	Windy

2 Weather Forecast (2)

Stadt	*Wetter*	*Temperaturen um 13 Uhr*
Berlin	Sonne	3
München	Wolkig	5
Paris	Regen	6
London	Neblig	7
Oslo	Schnee	- 4
Moskau	Schnee	- 1
Warschau	Sonne	4
Madrid	Sonne	7
Bonn	Wolkig	6
Rom	Sonne	13

1 Which city had the warmest weather?
2 Where would you least like to have been? Explain your answer.
3 What was the weather in (a) Moscow, (b) Warsaw, (c) Paris, (d) Munich?
4 At what time of day were these readings taken?

3 In the Town (1)

In the left-hand column are notices often seen in German towns. Match each notice with its English equivalent chosen from the right-hand column.

1	Verkehrsamt	A	Swimming-pool
2	Postamt	B	Cinema
3	Bibliothek	C	Hospital
4	Bahnhof	D	Church
5	Marktplatz	E	Library
6	Drogerie	F	Post office
7	Flughafen	G	Castle
8	Rathaus	H	Station
9	Kirche	I	Market-place
10	Dom	J	Airport
11	Kino	K	Town Hall
12	Schloß	L	Chemist's
13	Krankenhaus	M	Travel agency
14	Schwimmbad	N	Tourist information office
15	Reisebüro	O	Cathedral

4 Everyday Phrases

In the left-hand column are phrases often heard in Germany. Match each phrase with its English equivalent from the right-hand column.

1	Guten Tag	A	That is all
2	Entschuldigen Sie bitte	B	What would you like?
3	Danke schön	C	I do not understand
4	Auf Wiedersehen	D	How much is that?
5	Viel Spaß!	E	Goodbye
6	Gute Reise	F	How are you?
7	Gute Besserung	G	Thank you very much
8	Wieviel kostet das?	H	Anything else?
9	Was wünschen Sie?	I	I beg your pardon?
10	Wie bitte?	J	Excuse me, please
11	Sonst etwas?	K	Get well soon
12	Wie geht es Ihnen?	L	Good day
13	Verzeihung	M	Have a good time!
14	Ich verstehe nicht	N	Sorry
15	Das ist alles	O	Have a good journey!

Revision Test A

Give the meanings of these words and phrases chosen from exercises 1 - 4.

(a) Schnee
(b) stürmisch
(c) kalt
(d) wolkig
(e) Postamt
(f) Flughafen
(g) Schwimmbad
(h) Dom
(i) wieviel kostet das?
(j) Auf Wiedersehen

5 Where would you hear it? (1)

Study the ten remarks given below and then match each remark with the place where you would be most likely to hear it.

1 Ich möchte dreißig Liter Benzin.
2 Haben Sie bitte eine englische Zeitung?
3 Haben Sie etwas zu verzollen?
4 Ich fühle mich seekrank.
5 Zwei Pfund Kaffee und ein Pfund Zucker, bitte.
6 Ich möchte diesen Brief mit Luftpost schicken.
7 Ich möchte diese Schweinekoteletten, bitte.
8 Darf ich bitte die Speisekarte sehen?
9 Ich möchte eine Reise nach England buchen.
10 Von welchem Bahnsteig fährt der Zug nach Bonn?

A at the customs
B on a boat
C at a filling-station
D at a newsagent's
E at a post office
F at a grocery
G at a travel agency
H at a butcher's
I at a railway station
J in a restaurant

6 In the Town (2)

In the left-hand column are notices often seen in German towns. Match each notice with its English equivalent chosen from the right-hand column.

1	Einstieg nur vorn	A	Telephone
2	Fußgänger	B	Entry at your own risk
3	Abfälle	C	View of the sea
4	Betreten auf eigene Gefahr	D	Serve yourself to petrol
5	Bitte läuten	E	Special offer
6	Zahlen Sie an Kasse	F	Central heating
7	Friseur	G	Please ring
8	Sonderangebot	H	For sale
9	Ausfahrt freihalten	I	Pay at the cash-desk
10	Selbst tanken	J	Keep the exit clear
11	Fernsprecher	K	Enter at the front only
12	Zimmer mit Bad	L	Hairdresser
13	Zentralheizung	M	Litter
14	Blick auf die See	N	Pedestrians
15	Zu verkaufen	O	Rooms with a bath

7 Where would you hear it? (2)

Study the ten remarks below and then match each remark with the place where you would be most likely to hear it.

1. Darf ich bitte diese Jacke anprobieren?
2. Soll ich Öl und Wasser nachschauen oder den Luftdruck prüfen?
3. Die Obsttorten kosten drei Mark zwanzig das Stück. Wieviele Torten möchten Sie?
4. Haben Sie bitte ein Zimmer frei?
5. Vorsicht auf Gleis vier!
6. Befestigen Sie die Sicherheitsgurte. Wir landen in zehn Minuten in London.
7. Zwei Kilo Kartoffeln und ein Kilo Rosenkohl, bitte.
8. Wir stehen jetzt vor dem Rathaus. Hinter Ihnen ist das Schloss.
9. Passagiere für den Flug nach Hamburg, bitte am Flugsteig sieben melden.
10. Sie haben Kopfschmerze? Nehmen Sie diese Tabletten und kommen Sie bitte in zwei Wochen zurück.

A	at a railway station	F	at an airport
B	in an aircraft	G	in a confectioner's
C	in a clothes' store	H	at a greengrocer's
D	in the street	I	at the doctor's
E	at a filling-station	J	at a hotel

8 In the Town (3)

In the left-hand column below are notices often seen in German towns. Match each notice with its English equivalent chosen from the right-hand column.

1	Stadtmitte	A	School
2	Sparkasse	B	Toy shop
3	Schule	C	Baker's
4	Metzgerei	D	Delicatessen
5	Konditorei	E	Youth hostel
6	Hauptstraße	F	Savings bank
7	Hafen	G	Police
8	Blumenhandlung	H	Butcher's
9	Imbiß-stube	I	High street
10	Polizei	J	Underground railway
11	Feinkostladen	K	Confectioner's
12	U-Bahn	L	Florist's
13	Jugendherberge	M	Snack-bar
14	Spielwarengeschäft	N	Town-centre
15	Bäckerei	O	Harbour
16	Parkplatz	P	Diversion
17	Straße gesperrt	Q	To let
18	Nicht überholen	R	Road works
19	Straßenbau	S	Rooms with a shower
20	Kein Zutritt	T	Car park
21	Umleitung	U	No parking
22	Zu vermieten	V	No entry
23	Parken verboten	W	Road closed
24	Zimmer mit Dusche	X	Rooms with running water
25	Zimmer mit Fließwasser	Y	No overtaking

Revision Test B

Give the meanings of these words and phrases chosen from exercises 5-8.

(a) Benzin
(b) mit Luftpost
(c) Speisekarte
(d) Friseur
(e) Fußgänger
(f) Zahlen Sie an Kasse
(g) Fernsprecher
(h) Zentralheizung
(i) Kartoffeln
(j) Rathaus
(k) Stadtmitte
(l) Hauptstraße
(m) U-Bahn
(n) Jugendherberge
(o) Polizei

9 Where would you hear it? (3)

Study each remark and then choose the place where you would be most likely to hear it.

1 Ich möchte diesen Reisescheck wechseln.
(a) at the baker's
(b) in a bank
(c) at a post office
(d) at the chemist's

2 Möchten Sie ein Einzelzimmer oder ein Doppelzimmer?
(a) at a camp-site
(b) in a bedroom
(c) in a hotel
(d) at a restaurant

3 Wann beginnt die letzte Vorstellung?
(a) at a railway station
(b) at a butcher's
(c) at a florist's
(d) at a theatre

4 Ich möchte einen Strandkorb mieten.
(a) at the seaside
(b) in the countryside
(c) in the town-centre
(d) in the mountains

5 Ich möchte dieses Telegramm aufgeben.
(a) at a café
(b) at a post office
(c) in an aircraft
(d) at a filling station

6 Geben Sie mir bitte zweihundert Gramm Leberwurst.
(a) at a supermarket check-out
(b) at a travel agency
(c) at a butcher's
(d) in a taxi

7 Ist hier noch jemand ohne Fahrschein?
(a) in a tram
(b) in a lift
(c) on a motorway
(d) in a café

8 Guten Tag, Ihren Paß, bitte.
(a) at a garage
(b) on a farm
(c) in a shop
(d) at a border check-point

9 Einmal zweiter Klasse nach Stuttgart bitte. Hin und zurück. Muß ich umsteigen?
(a) at a railway ticket-office
(b) in a bus
(c) in a classroom
(d) on a railway platform

10 Zweimal Suppe, einmal Jägerschnitzel, einmal Omelett, ein Viertel Weißwein und ein kleines Bier, bitte.
(a) at home
(b) in a restaurant
(c) in a supermarket
(d) at a zoo

10 At a Restaurant

HOTEL-RESTAURANT UND CAFE SCHMIDT

Besitzer: Peter Schmidt

Speisekarte

Erbsensuppe	**2,00**
Tomatensuppe	**2,10**
Omelett, gemischter Salat	**4,75**
Fischsalat	**3,50**
Gemischte kalte Platte mit Butter und Brot	**5,00**
Käseplatte, Butter und Brot	**4,40**
Schweinekotelett mit Salat und Bratkartoffeln	**5,70**
Huhn auf Reis, Spargel oder Champignons	**6,40**
Gebratenes Rindfleisch mit Pommes Frites und Bohnen	**7,20**
Roastbeef, kalt, Bratkartoffeln und Salat	**5,45**
Wiener Schnitzel mit Röstkartoffeln	**7,00**
Forelle, gemischter Salat, Salzkartoffeln	**8,00**
Kuchen, pro Stück	**1,80**
Kännchen Kaffee mit Schlagsahne	**2,00**
Eine Scheibe Ananas	**-, 80**
Obst, pro Stück	**-, 50**
Eis	**1,80**
Obstsalat	**2,70**
Bier (0, 5 l.)	**ab 1,80**
Mineralwasser	**1,20**
Obstsaft	**1,10**
Rotwein, Weißwein, das Glas	**ab 2,10**

Bedienung: 10%

1 Which soup is more expensive — pea or tomato?
2 What is served with omelette?
3 How much does the pork chop cost and with what is it served?
4 How much does the chicken dish cost?

5 Which dishes are served with fried potatoes and which with roast potatoes?
6 Calculate the bills for the following clients of the restaurant:

Client A orders pea soup, chicken with rice, and the pineapple dessert.
Client B orders tomato soup, trout, an ice and a glass of the cheapest beer.
Client C orders an omelette, followed by fruit salad, and then a mineral water.
Client D orders veal with roast potatoes, followed by a fruit, and drinks two glasses of the cheapest white wine.

Do not forget to add any service charge which may have to be included on the bills.

11 Notices at a Railway Station

In the left-hand column are notices often seen on German railway stations. Match each notice with its English equivalent chosen from the right-hand column.

1	Ankunft	A	Left luggage office
2	Fahrkarten	B	Buses
3	Auskunft	C	Lost property office
4	Abfahrt	D	No smoking compartment
5	Busse	E	Tickets
6	Fundbüro	F	Refreshments
7	Verbindungen	G	Departure
8	Nichtraucher	H	Arrival
9	Gepäckaufbewahrung	I	Connections
10	Erfrischungen	J	Information
11	Hauptbahnhof	K	Main lines
12	Warteraum	L	Tickets for reserved seats
13	Taxistand	M	Platform two
14	Platzkarten	N	To the trains
15	S-Bahn	O	Main station
16	Zu den Zügen	P	Do not lean out
17	Gleis zwei	Q	Taxi-rank
18	Nicht hinauslehnen	R	Waiting room
19	Nicht öffnen bevor der Zug hält	S	Suburban trains
20	Hauptstrecken	T	Do not open before the train stops

12 At the Supermarket

ALBRECHT
Kaiserplatz

SONDERANGEBOTE – NUR DIESE WOCHE

Eier (6, 12)	1.20, 2.40
Bier, 6 x 0.2 Literflaschen	2.98
1 Kilo Äpfel	1.20
100g Kaffee	2.40
500ml Mineralwasser	-. 25
Liter Whisky	22.10

	UNSER PREIS
Reis, 500g Paket	1.20
1 Kilo Kartoffeln	1.20
Bockwurst, 300g	5.30
Blumenkohl, $\frac{1}{2}$ Kilo	-. 99
1 Kilo Erbsen	1.60
$\frac{1}{2}$ Kilo Pilze	2.70
1 Kilo Tomaten	1.80
1 Kilo Zwiebeln	1.20

GEÖFFNET:
sechs Wochentage von 9.00
bis 17.30, Freitagabend
geöffnet bis 20.00
U-BAHNHALTESTELLE:
Rathaus

1 For how long will these special offers last?
2 Calculate the bills for these four orders:
 (a) a kilo of potatoes, a kilo of tomatoes and six eggs,
 (b) a dozen eggs, six bottles of mineral water and a kilo of apples,
 (c) a kilo of peas, a packet of rice and six bottles of beer,
 (d) a kilo of onions, a half-kilo of mushrooms and a bottle of whisky.
3 On how many days of the week is the supermarket open?
4 For how many hours is the supermarket open on (a) Mondays, (b) Fridays, (c) Saturdays?
5 When is late-night shopping at this supermarket?
6 Near which important building is the closest underground station?

Assignment

Find out:
(a) how many grams make one kilogram,
(b) how many grams are equivalent to one pound,
(c) how many pounds make one kilogram.

Revision Test C

Match the following words and phrases from exercises 9-12 with their English equivalents.

1	Einzelzimmer	A	Service charge
2	Leberwurst	B	Cakes
3	Ihren Paß, bitte	C	No-smoking compartment
4	Muß ich umsteigen?	D	Mineral water
5	Weißwein	E	Platform two
6	Kuchen	F	Do I have to change?
7	Kaffee	G	Cauliflower
8	Mineralwasser	H	Single room
9	Bedienung	I	Special offers
10	Fahrkarten	J	Coffee
11	Nichtraucher	K	Liver sausage
12	Gleis zwei	L	Tickets
13	Sonderangebote	M	Your passport, please
14	Blumenkohl	N	Open
15	Geöffnet	O	White wine

13 Reading a Newspaper

Seiten	**Inhalt**
2, 3, 4	Nachrichten aus aller Welt
5	Politische Nachrichten
5	Wetterbericht
7	Leserbriefe
10	Roman in Folgen
12, 13	Sportnachrichten
14, 15	Theater und Kino
16	Finanznachrichten
17	Buchempfehlungen
18	Humor

1 How many pages of world news does this newspaper carry?
2 What can you find on page 5?
3 On which page(s) is the sports news?
4 Where would you find information about films and shows?
5 On which page are books reviewed?
6 Where would you find cartoons?
7 What would you find on page 10?
8 Where is the financial news?
9 On which page are letters to the newspaper from its readers?

14 A Tourist Asks the Way

‚Das Schwimmbad? Ja. Gehen Sie hundert Meter geradeaus und dann gehen Sie bei der Ampel rechts. Nach fünfzig Metern sehen Sie das Krankenhaus.

‚Gehen Sie vor dem Krankenhaus nach links, bis Sie zur Polizeiwache kommen. Das Schwimmbad befindet sich hinter der Polizeiwache.'

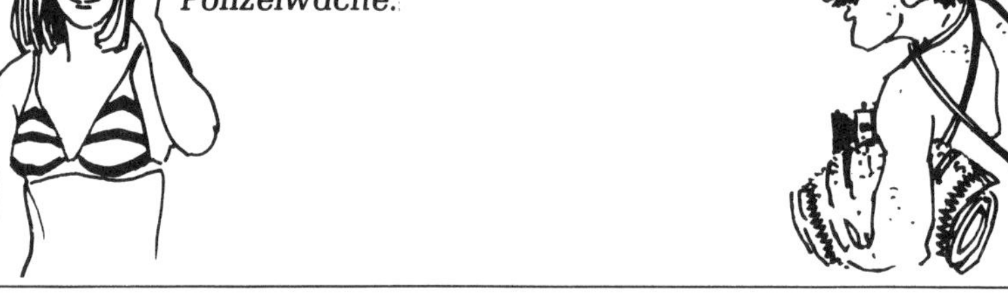

1 How far away from the speaker are the traffic lights?
2 What must the tourist do at the traffic lights?
3 How far from the lights is the hospital?
4 What must the tourist do in front of the hospital?
5 Which building will the tourist see next?
6 Where does the swimming-pool lie?

15 At the Swimming Pool

STÄDTISCHES SCHWIMMBAD

PREISE:

Erwachsene (über 16)	2 DM
Block mit zwanzig Karten	30 DM
Kinder (unter 16)	1.50 DM
Block mit zwanzig Karten	20 DM
Blöcke mit dreißig Karten für die ganze Familie	25 DM

GEÖFFNET:

Montag, Dienstag, Mittwoch, Donnerstag, Freitag
von 7.00 bis 18.30

Für die Öffentlichkeit ausschließlich reserviert:

Mittwochs	von 14.00 bis 17.00
Samstags	von 14.00 bis 20.00
Sonntags	von 9.00 bis 12.00
und	von 15.00 bis 19.00

1 At what age must one pay the adult tariff?
2 Explain what may be purchased for thirty marks.
3 How much would a child expect to save by buying a book of twenty tickets?
4 On which days of the week is the pool reserved exclusively for the public?
5 What is the normal closing-time at the pool? How does this change at weekends?
6 For how many hours is the pool reserved exclusively for the public on Sundays?

16 Everyday Notices (1)

In the left-hand column are notices frequently seen in Germany. Match each notice with its English equivalent chosen from the right-hand column.

1	Ausgang	A	Wait
2	Einbahnstraße	B	Private
3	Rechts halten	C	No entry
4	Fußgängerzone	D	One-way street
5	Privat	E	Free entrance
6	Eingang	F	Pedestrian precinct
7	Zutritt verboten	G	Exit
8	Eintritt frei	H	Entrance
9	Warten	I	Danger
10	Gefahr	J	Keep to the right
11	Nur für Radfahrer	K	Special offer
12	Vorsicht! bissiger Hund	L	Camping area
13	Drücken	M	Motorway service area
14	Autobahn	N	Press
15	Ziehen	O	Money-changing office
16	Raststätte	P	For cyclists only
17	Sonderangebot	Q	Danger of death
18	Lebensgefahr	R	Beware of the dog
19	Geldwechsel	S	Pull
20	Zeltplatz	T	Motorway
21	Vorsicht! Glas!	U	Sale
22	Zoll	V	Customs
23	Ausverkauf	W	Beware! Glass!

Revision Test D

Give the meanings of these words chosen from exercises 13-16.

(a) Nachrichten
(b) Kino
(c) Eingang
(d) Gefahr
(e) Autobahn
(f) Geldwechsel
(g) Krankenhaus
(h) Erwachsene
(i) reserviert
(j) Sonntags

17 Sale in a Department Store (1)

Karstadt

Vom 6. bis 20. Januar

Sensationelle Preise!

Tausende von Luxusgegenständen!

Kleider
Reiseartikel
Möbel
Parfüm
Elektroartikel
Glaswaren
Autoausstattungen
Bücher
Teppiche
Kochgeschirr

Täglich von 10.00 bis 18.30 (außer Montagen)

1 For how many hours a day is the store open?
2 On which day of the week is the store closed?
3 This advertisement mentions ten departments in which prices are reduced. List as many as you can in English.

18 Television Programmes

Drittes Programm – Nord 3

14.00 Guten Tag!
Ein Programm für die Hausfrau

15.00 Der Letzte Gefangene
Ein Kriminalfilm

16.30 Zeichnentrickfilme

17.00 Nachrichten

17.10 Regionalnachrichten
(mit dem Wetterbericht)

17.30 Im Urwald Verirrt
Film über eine Expedition zum südamerikanischen Urwald

18.00 Richtig oder Falsch?
Eine Quiz-sendung

18.45 Bericht aus Bonn
Politische Tagesneuigkeiten

19.30 Internationaler Fußball
Österreich gegen Westdeutschland
Liveübertragung aus Wien

21.15 Nachrichten

21.30 Der vermißte Mann
Ein Spionagefilm

23.45 Letzte Nachrichten
(mit dem Wetterbericht)

23.50 Sendeschluß

1 What kind of programme is 'Guten Tag'?
2 At what time are cartoons being shown?
3 At what times during the day can viewers see the news?
4 At what time is a quiz programme transmitted?
5 How long does the programme of political news last?
6 Which teams are competing in the football match?
7 When can viewers see the weather forecast?
8 Classify each of these programmes under one of the headings supplied in the survey below.

Popular Television Programmes

Here are the results of a survey which asked German television viewers about their favourite programmes. The different kinds of programme are listed in order of popularity.

Programm-Kategorien	**% der Zuschauer**
Aktuelle Nachrichten	69
Spielfilme und Krimis	67
Unterhaltung (Show und Quiz)	62
Fernsehspiele und Theaterstücke	55
Sport	47
Western-Serien	43
Politische Sendungen	37

1 What percentage of viewers regularly watches the news?
2 In what position in the table are television plays?
3 By how great a percentage are detective films more popular than political broadcasts?
4 Rewrite the order of these programme categories according to your own preference.

19 Extract from a Railway Timetable

Look at the timetable opposite.

1 For where does the first train after midday leave?
2 Which is the first train of the afternoon which stops at Unna?
3 From which platform does the first afternoon train to Cologne leave?
4 Which is the first train to Düsseldorf?
5 How long does the journey to Aachen take?
6 On how many days of the week does the 12.45 to Düsseldorf run?
7 Which is the first Sunday train to Soest?
8 How long does the journey to Fulda take?
9 Which is the only train on this timetable travelling outside Germany?
10 Which train would you take if you wished to (a) arrive in Aachen in the late afternoon, (b) reach Dortmund shortly after lunch, (c) travel to Kassel?

ABFAHRT		
Zeit:	**In Richtung nach:**	**Gleis:**
12.01	MINDEN	3
12.13	KÖLN HBF. Ankunft 13.59 Hält nicht in Unna	3
12.25	KÖLN HBF. Ankunft 14.02 über Unna, Dortmund, Essen, Duisburg, Düsseldorf	6
12.38	AACHEN HBF. Ankunft 15.51 über Dortmund, Duisburg, Krefeld	4
12.45	DÜSSELDORF HBF. außer Samstagen	5
13.10	PADERBORN HBF. über Soest nicht an Sonntagen	3
13.26	FULDA Ankunft 18.48 über Paderborn und Kassel	7
13.45	PARIS-NORD über Dortmund 14.06 — Essen 14.47 — Köln 15.58 — Aachen 16.58	8
14.02	SOEST täglich außer Samstagen	2
14.27	HANNOVER Ankunft 15.59 über Lüneburg	2

20 Sale in a Department Store (2)

HERTEN

macht Ausverkauf

Sonderangebote –
bis einschließlich 3. Dezember
20% Ermäßigung an Hunderten von Artikeln in allen Abteilungen

Artikel	Alter Preis	Neuer Preis
Anzüge	~~165~~	130 DM
Röcke	~~69~~	56 DM
Herrenhemden	~~49~~	40 DM
Schlafanzüge	~~30~~	24 DM
Kindermäntel	~~212~~	170 DM
Lederhandtaschen	~~60~~	48 DM
Bügeleisen	~~85~~	68 DM
Baumwolleintuch, 180 x 300 cm.	~~25~~	20 DM
Wolldecken, 200 x 240 cm.	~~100~~	80 DM
Daunendecken, 140 x 150 cm.	~~75~~	60 DM

1 Will this sale be open on December 3rd?
2 By how much have the following items been reduced:
   (a) a handbag?
   (b) a pair of pyjamas?
   (c) an iron?
   (d) an eiderdown?
3 What would be the total cost of:
   (a) a shirt and a suit?
   (b) a sheet and a blanket?
   (c) a skirt and a child's coat?

Revision Test E

Give the meanings of these words and phrases chosen from exercises 17-20.

(a) Reiseartikel
(b) Kochgeschirr
(c) täglich
(d) außer Montagen
(e) Gleis
(f) Ankunft
(g) 20% Ermäßigung
(h) Wetterbericht
(i) Österreich
(j) Sendeschluß

Progress Test

All the words and phrases in this test have been met in the first twenty exercises. How many can you understand?

1 Sonne
2 windig
3 Regen
4 Warschau
5 Marktplatz
6 Reisebüro
7 wie geht es Ihnen?
8 haben Sie etwas zu verzollen?
9 Friseur
10 zu verkaufen
11 Jugendherberge
12 kein Zutritt
13 Dusche
14 Hafen
15 zweimal Suppe
16 Obstsaft
17 gemischter Salat
18 nicht öffnen bevor der Zug hält
19 Warteraum
20 Bockwurst
21 Ausgang
22 an Feiertagen geschlossen
23 Kinder
24 Anzüge
25 Herrenhemden

21 A Weekend Holiday

— an einem verlängerten Wochenende
— mit einem deutschen Reiseleiter

NEW YORK

Abfahrt	Frankfurt am Freitag dem 11. November um 12.00 Uhr
Ankunft	Frankfurt am Dienstag dem 15. November um 9.10 Uhr
Preis	995 DM (pro Person in einem Doppelzimmer)
Der Preis enthält:	* Direktflug * Alle Überfahrten * Unterkunft im Hotel Summit * Frühstück * Stadtrundfahrt durch New York mit deutschem Reiseleiter

Erfragen Sie Einzelheiten im Reisebüro Wagner, Hamburg

1 From which city does this tour leave?
2 Do passengers return in the morning, afternoon or evening?
3 What would be the cost of taking this tour for a husband and wife?
4 What is included in the price of the tour?
5 What is not included in the price and could add a good deal more to the cost?

22 Holiday Accommodation

Look at the accommodation advertisement opposite.

1 Use an atlas to locate the town of Heilbronn. In which West German state does it lie?
2 Would you expect to find the rooms in this Gasthof old-fashioned in appearance? Explain your answer.
3 With what are all rooms equipped?
4 How easily can one park a car at this Gasthof? Explain your answer.

Assignment
Compile a similar advertisement for a Gasthof of your own.

Während Ihres Aufenthalts in Heilbronn

besuchen Sie den . . . 

einen der ältesten Gasthöfe der Gegend
erbaut um 1527
Zimmer neuzeitlich
Telefon in allen Zimmern
Fünfundsiebzig Betten
Duschen Bäder
Vorzügliche Küche Erlesene Weine
Parkmöglichkeit 80m links und rechts vom Löwen
Eigentümer: Fritz Weber
Telefon, 4 39 63

23 Sale Bargains

WOLFGANG FERDINAND

Elektrische Geräte zu Spottpreisen!

Waschmaschinen ab	298 DM	Autoradios ab	76 DM
Kühlschränke ab	175 DM	Farbfernseher ab	1225 DM
Gefrierschränke ab	359 DM	Rasenmäher ab	135 DM
Staubsauger ab	125 DM	Haartrockner ab	30 DM
Kassettenrekorder ab	99 DM	Bügeleisen ab	49 DM
Plattenspieler ab	138 DM		

Offen an sieben Wochentagen 9.00 — 18.00
(Sonntags 10.00 — 17.00)

Lübeckerstraße, Hamburg

U-Bahnhaltestelle: Klosterstern

1 On how many days of the week is this store open?
2 For how many hours is the store open on (a) Mondays, (b) Sundays?
3 List in English as many of the goods on sale in this store as you can.
4 What is Klosterstern?

REISEBÜRO WAGNER

Sonderreisen:

Kopenhagen	Wochenendreise, drei Tage, Hotel mit Frühstück und Stadtrundfahrt, Flug ab Hamburg	**550 DM**
Lissabon	Eine Woche, Hotel mit Halbpension, Stadtrundfahrt, Flug ab Frankfurt	**900 DM**
Norwegen	Schiffsreise, norwegische Fjorde, dreizehn Tage Vollpension, Flug ab Hamburg	**2200 DM**
Mallorca	Palma, Wochenendreise mit zwei Übernachtungen und Frühstück, Luxus-Hotel Valparaiso Palace, Flug ab Frankfurt	**750 DM**
Schwarzmeer-Kreuzfahrt	Fünfzehn Tage, Vollpension, Flug ab Frankfurt	**4500 DM**
Kanarische Inseln	Fünfzehn Tage mit Frühstück, Appartment am Strand, Flug ab Frankfurt	**1700 DM**
London	Wochenendreise, drei Tage, Hotel mit Frühstück und Stadtrundfahrt, Flug ab Köln	**300 DM**
USA	Naturwunder der USA, vierundzwanzig-Tage-Rundreise mit deutscher Reiseleitung zu den schönsten Nationalparks der USA. Inklusiv aller Flüge, Mahlzeiten, und Unterbringung in sehr guten Hotels, Flug ab Frankfurt	**6500 DM**

Buchen Sie noch heute Ihre Traumferien!

24 Exciting Holidays

Look at the travel agency advertisement opposite.

1 How many days does the Copenhagen holiday last? Which meal(s) does the cost include?
2 Which of these holiday offer(s) include(s) a tour of the city?
3 How many daily meals does the Lisbon holiday include?
4 Are all meals included on the Norwegian holiday?
5 How many nights will tourists spend in a hotel on the Majorcan holiday?
6 What is the cost of the Black Sea cruise?
7 Where are the Canary Islands apartments situated?
8 Which holidays do not begin with a flight from Frankfurt?
9 How long does the American holiday last?
10 What does the cost of the American holiday include?

Revision Test F

Match the following words and phrases from exercises 21-24 with their English equivalents.

1	Reiseleiter	A	Inn
2	Abfahrt	B	Refrigerator
3	Frühstück	C	Half-board
4	Stadtrundfahrt	D	Hair-drier
5	Gasthof	E	Weekend excursion
6	Waschmaschine	F	Boat trip
7	Kühlschrank	G	Tour leader
8	Farbfernseher	H	Flight
9	Haartrockner	I	Tour of the town
10	Halbpension	J	Meals
11	Vollpension	K	Departure
12	Wochenendreise	L	Full-board
13	Schiffsreise	M	Washing machine
14	Flug	N	Breakfast
15	Mahlzeiten	O	Colour television set

25 Clothing Sale

Herrenbekleidung

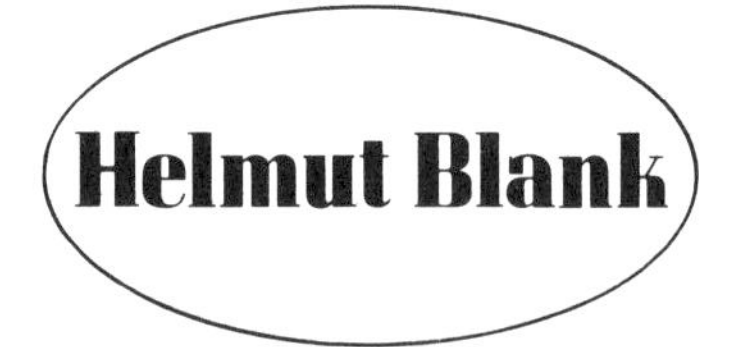

Frankfurt-am-Main

Winterschlußverkauf

Alle Kleidungsartikel bis zu 30% ermäßigt!

	Normalpreis	*Unser Preis*
Mäntel	**270**	**189 DM**
Hemden	**35**	**25 DM**
Krawatten	**12**	**9 DM**
Jacken	**160**	**120 DM**
Handschuhe	**40**	**30 DM**
Herrenhosen	**50**	**35 DM**
Regenmäntel	**120**	**99 DM**
Regenschirme	**20**	**15 DM**
Hüte	**45**	**35 DM**

Der Schlußverkauf beginnt am Montag dem 4. Januar um 9.15 Uhr.
Ganztägig geöffnet von 9.15 bis 17.30
(Samstags von 9.15 bis 13.30)
Der Schlußverkauf wird bis zum 16. Januar dauern

1 By how much have the following items been reduced: (a) gloves, (b) ties, (c) umbrellas?
2 Calculate the total cost of a hat, an umbrella and a raincoat.
3 Calculate the total cost of a jacket and an overcoat.
4 Which items have been reduced by the full 30%?
5 On which day of the week does the sale begin?
6 For how many hours a day is the store open during the week?

26 A Football League Table

Look at the table opposite.

(A) 1. How many points have Cologne dropped this season?
2. How many teams have lost four matches?

Mannschaft	gespielt	gewonnen	unent-schieden	verloren	Tore	Punkte
Köln	15	10	1	4	47-24	21-9
Mönchen-gladbach	15	8	3	4	34-23	19-11
Kaiserslautern	15	8	3	4	28-23	19-11
Düsseldorf	15	8	2	5	24-18	18-12
Schalke 04	15	7	4	4	23-22	18-12
Dortmund	15	8	1	6	29-28	17-13
Stuttgart	15	7	2	6	21-20	16-14
Hamburg	15	7	2	6	25-26	16-14
Braunschweig	15	8	0	7	22-23	16-14
Hertha BSC	15	6	4	5	20-23	16-14
Frankfurt	15	7	1	7	30-26	15-15
Duisburg	15	5	4	6	29-28	14-16
Saarbrücken	15	5	4	6	21-28	14-16
Bremen	15	5	3	7	20-28	13-17
Bayern München	15	4	4	7	31-34	12-18
Bochum	15	4	3	8	16-18	11-19
St Pauli	15	4	2	9	25-34	10-20
1860 München	15	1	3	11	13-32	5-25

3. Which team has not drawn any matches?
4. How many teams have lost more matches than they have won?
5. Why are Saarbrücken lower in the table than Duisburg?
6. Which teams have the best defensive record in the league?
7. Which team has conceded more than twice as many goals as it has scored?

(**B**) The next matches to be played in the Bundesliga ended in the following scores:

Stuttgart	1 : 0	Köln
Mönchen-gladbach	2 : 1	Hamburg
St Pauli	0 : 3	Düsseldorf
Frankfurt	1 : 1	Bayern München
1860 München	0 : 0	Braunschweig
Hertha BSC	2 : 3	Schalke 04
Bochum	0 : 2	Dortmund

Rewrite the league table as it appeared after these results.

27 International Football

Gruppe 1	**2 Juni**	Ungarn - Argentinien Frankreich - Italien
	6 Juni	Argentinien - Frankreich Italien - Ungarn
	10 Juni	Italien - Argentinien Frankreich - Ungarn
Gruppe 2	**1 Juni**	Westdeutschland - Polen (Eröffnungsspiel)
	2 Juni	Tunesien - Mexiko
	6 Juni	Polen - Tunesien Mexiko-Westdeutschland
	8 Juni	Polen - Mexiko
	10 Juni	Tunesien - Westdeutschland
Gruppe 3	**3 Juni**	Spanien - Österreich Schweden - Brasilien
	7 Juni	Österreich - Schweden Brasilien - Spanien
	11 Juni	Schweden - Spanien Brasilien - Österreich
Gruppe 4	**3 Juni**	Peru - Schottland Iran - Holland
	7 Juni	Schottland - Iran Holland - Peru
	11 Juni	Peru - Iran Schottland - Holland

Die zwei besten Teams jeder Gruppe qualifizieren sich für die zweite Runde (14, 18, 21 Juni).

24 Juni Spiel um den dritten und vierten Platz

26 Juni Endspiel

1 How many matches do all teams play in the first round?
2 When is the first match?
3 Which is the only team from the United Kingdom involved in this tournament?

4 Which team does West Germany meet in the first round?
5 How many teams qualify for the second round?
6 On how many dates will the second round matches be played?
7 What will teams be competing for on June 24th?
8 When is the Final?

28 Everyday Notices (2)

In the left-hand column are notices frequently seen in Germany. Match each notice with its English equivalent, chosen from the right-hand column.

1	Sackgasse	A	Do not lean bicycles here
2	Hier kein Übergang	B	Wet paint
3	Dieses Geschäft wird um 18 Uhr geschlossen	C	Cul-de-sac
4	Fahrräder nicht anlehnen	D	Do not cross here
5	Frisch gestrichen	E	This shop closes at 6 p.m.
6	Kein Einstieg	F	Dogs must be on a lead
7	Motor abstellen	G	Freshly polished
8	Bitte andere Tür benutzen	H	Emergency exit
9	Licht einschalten	I	No entry
10	Frisch gebohnert	J	Inflammable
11	Für Garderobe wird nicht gehaftet	K	Use the other door, please
12	Das Betreten des Rasens ist verboten	L	Switch off engine
13	Notausstieg	M	Switch on the light
14	Hunde an der Leine führen	N	No responsibility accepted for safety of coats
15	Feuergefährlich	O	Do not walk on the lawn
16	Herren	P	Open
17	Gasthof	Q	Occupied
18	Berühren verboten	R	Reserved
19	Offen	S	Gentlemen
20	Ausverkauft	T	Self-service
21	Damen	U	Drinking water
22	Besetzt	V	Do not touch
23	Reserviert	W	Inn
24	Selbstbedienung	X	Sold out
25	Trinkwasser	Y	Ladies

Revision Test G

Give the meanings of these words chosen from exercises 25-28.

(a) Westdeutschland
(b) Regenschirm
(c) Hüte
(d) Frankreich
(e) Schottland
(f) Krawatte
(g) feuergefährlich
(h) Notausstieg
(i) Damen
(j) Selbstbedienung

29 A Tour of the Town

STADTRUNDFAHRT

Täglich	außer Sonntag
Dauer	dreieinhalb Stunden

Die Fahrt beinhaltet Besuche zum Dom, zum Opernhaus, zum städtischen Museum und zum Hafen.

Busse fahren zu folgenden Zeiten:

9.00 11.30 13.15 15.15

Treffpunkt	vor dem Rathaus	
Preis	Erwachsene	12 DM
	Kinder unter 14	8 DM

Karten können in jedem städtischen Reisebüro im voraus erworben werden.

1 On how many days of the week does the tour run?
2 How long does the tour last?
3 To which four places does the tour include a visit?
4 How many tours operate (a) during the morning, (b) during the afternoon?
5 From where do the tours begin?
6 Calculate the cost of taking this tour for:
(a) a mother and her seven-years-old son,
(b) a father, mother and their sixteen-years-old daughter,
(c) two twelve-years-old girls.
7 Where may tickets be purchased in advance?

30 Booking into a German Hotel

‚Guten Abend. Ich heiße Schmidt. Haben Sie bitte ein freies Enzelzimmer?'

‚Ja, Herr Schmidt. Zur Zeit haben wir drei freie Einzelzimmer. Eines befindet sich im ersten Stock. Es hat eine Dusche und kostet vierzig Mark.

‚Das zweite Zimmer liegt im dritten Stock und hat ein Badezimmer. Dieses Zimmer kostet etwas mehr, nämlich fünfzig Mark, hat aber ausserdem Telephon und Fernsehen.

‚Das dritte Zimmer ist im fünften Stock. Das Hotel hat selbstverständlich einen Aufzug. Das Zimmer hat Balkon und eine herrliche Aussicht zum See. Dieses Zimmer kostet sechzig Mark.

‚Alle Zimmer haben Zentralheizung und die Preise sind Inklusivpreise.'

‚Gut. Ich nehme das Zimmer im fünften Stock mit Aussicht zum See. Ich bleibe voraussichtlich drei Tage hier und werde Mittwoch abreisen.'

1 What kind of room would the visitor like?
2 How many rooms of this kind does the hotel have available?
3 How much does the first floor room cost?
4 How much more expensive is the room on the third floor? What do you think accounts for its being more costly?
5 Where is the third room?
6 How much does the third room cost?
7 What are all rooms equipped with?
8 Is a service charge included in the prices of the rooms?
9 Which room does the visitor choose, and why do you think he takes this one?
10 For how long does the visitor expect to stay at the hotel?

31 Bank Robbery (1)

Gestern nachmittag **kam ein** Mann in eine Stuttgarter **Bank** und legte einen Briefumschlag auf den Schaltertisch.

Auf dem Briefumschlag waren diese Worte zu lesen: **‚Dies ist ein Überfall! Füllen Sie diesen Umschlag mit Banknoten!'**

Der Mann hatte keine Pistole, aber er hatte seine Hand in der Tasche seiner Jacke. Der Bankbeamte übergab ihm fünftausend Mark, und der Eindringling verließ die Bank so unauffällig wie er gekommen war.

1 When did this incident occur?
2 What did the man place on the counter?
3 What was the cashier ordered to do?
4 Explain how the cashier was deceived.
5 How much money was stolen?

32 Bank Robbery (2)

Drei maskierte Räuber, mit Maschinenpistolen bewaffnet, raubten gestern eine Bank in der Frankfurter Innenstadt aus.

Sie zwangen die Bankangestellten, den Safe zu öffnen und sich dann unter die Tische zu legen.

Mit hunderttausend gestohlenen D-Mark entflohen die Räuber in einem weißen Opel Kadett.

Die Frankfurter Polizei meint die Autonummer zu kennen.

1. When was the bank robbed?
2. How many robbers were involved?
3. What were the robbers carrying?
4. What two things did the robbers force the bank employees to do?
5. How much money was stolen?
6. What suggests that the police are already on the trail of the robbers?

Revision Test H

Give the meanings of these words and phrases chosen from exercises 29-32.

(a) Opernhaus
(b) Treffpunkt
(c) Preis
(d) im ersten Stock
(e) Badezimmer
(f) Mittwoch
(g) Banknoten
(h) Jacke
(i) Innenstadt
(j) Räuber

33 Booking into a German Hotel (2)

Look at the letter opposite.

1. On which dates (a) was a letter written to this hotel, (b) did the hotel write its letter in reply, (c) does the client intend to arrive at the hotel, (d) does the client intend to leave?
2. How many rooms does the hotel still have available?
3. Explain the terms Halbpension and Vollpension.
4. On which floor of the hotel are the available rooms?
5. Calculate the bills for the following guests:
   (a) a married couple in a double room staying three nights and taking only breakfast in the hotel,
   (b) two friends staying in the smaller room for four nights and taking only breakfast in the hotel,

(c) a young man staying in the hotel on full board terms for six nights,

(d) a young lady staying in the hotel on half board terms for two nights.

6 Is a service charge already included in the prices quoted in the letter?

7 How far away from the River Rhine is the hotel?

8 How often are bus excursions operated and to where do they run?

Hotel zum Schwarzen Pferd

Berlinerstraße 7
Bingen
den 15. Juli

Sehr geehrter Herr MacDonald!

Ich habe Ihren Brief vom 3. Juli dankend erhalten.

Unser Hotel hat nur zwei Zimmer, die vom 20. bis 28. August noch frei sind:

Ein Doppelzimmer mit Toilette, und ein kleines Zimmer mit zwei Betten und Waschbecken. Diese Zimmer befinden sich im zweiten Stock.

Unser Übernachtungstarif:
Doppelzimmer mit Frühstück - täglich 65 DM
Kleines Zimmer mit Frühstück - täglich 55 DM
oder
Vollpension für eine Person- täglich 80 DM
Halbpension für eine Person- täglich 65 DM
(inklusiv Bedienung)

Das Hotel befindet sich nur dreihundert Meter vom Rhein entfernt. Wir haben ein großes Schwimmbad, und es gibt die Möglichkeit, die Schlösser und Weinberge mit den vielen täglichen Autobusausflügen zu besichtigen.

In Erwartung auf Ihre baldige Antwort,
Hochachtungsvoll,

Blechstein

34 Booking into a German Hotel (3)

Hotel Alpenrose

Garmisch-Partenkirchen

Familienname ____________________

Vorname (n) ____________________

Alter ____________________

Geburtsdatum ____________________

Staatsangehörigkeit ____________________

Beruf ____________________

Wohnort ____________________

Unterschrift ____________________

On arriving at a German hotel you are requested to complete *das Formular.*

Make a copy of the form illustrated here and then complete it with your own personal details.

35 A Presidential Visit

Der Präsident der Vereinigten Staaten wird heute abend in Warschau ankommen.

Warschau ist die erste Stadt, die er bei seinem neun-Tage-Aufenthalt in Europa und Asien besuchen wird.

1 Which country's President is mentioned in this news item?
2 Where will the President arrive this evening?
3 How long will the President's tour last?
4 Which continent other than Europe will the President visit?

Assignment

(a) Use an atlas to locate the city mentioned in this news report.
(b) How far from West Germany is this city?
(c) How far away from Russia does this city lie?

36 An Airline Pilot Speaks

'Guten Morgen, meine sehr verehrten Damen und Herren, hier spricht Flugkapitän Koenig. Wir fliegen in einer Höhe von zehntausend Metern über Frankreich. Wir werden New York in sechs Stunden erreichen. Währenddessen werden Sie von unseren Stewardessen mit Getränken, Zigaretten und Süßigkeiten bedient. In etwa drei Stunden wird Ihnen eine warme Mahlzeit gereicht werden. Das Wetter in New York ist zur Zeit bewölkt aber warm. Es hat zweiundzwanzig Grad. Ich wünsche Ihnen im Namen des ganzen Personals eine angenehme Reise und danke Ihnen für Ihre Aufmerksamkeit.'

1 At what height is the aircraft flying?
2 Over which country is the aircraft flying?
3 When will the aircraft land in New York?
4 What three things will the stewardesses serve?
5 What will be served in three hours' time?
6 What is the weather like in New York?
7 What is the temperature in New York?

37 Announcement at a Railway Station

'Der Zug, der um 14.20 in Köln abgefahren ist, wird in drei Minuten auf Gleis fünf ankommen.

'Der Zug, der um 15.10 in München abgefahren ist, wird mit zehn Minuten Verspätung auf Gleis zwei ankommen.

'Reisende, die mit dem Zug nach Stuttgart, Abfahrt 17.05, fahren, werden gebeten, mit Ihrer Fahrkarte zum Schalter drei zu kommen und dann sofort einzusteigen.

'Reisende nach Karlsruhe: nehmen Sie bitte in den letzten zwei Wagen Platz. In diesem Zug befindet sich ein Speisewagen. Wir wünschen Ihnen angenehme Reise!'

1 Where will the train from Cologne arrive?
2 When will the Cologne train arrive?
3 How late will the train from Munich be?
4 At which platform will the train from Munich arrive?
5 What two things are passengers for Stuttgart asked to do?
6 Where must passengers for Karlsruhe sit?
7 What will the Karlsruhe train comprise?

Revision Test I

Match the following words and phrases chosen from exercises 33-37 with their English equivalents.

1	Doppelzimmer	A	Date of birth
2	Waschbecken	B	United States
3	Vorname	C	ten minutes late
4	Geburtsdatum	D	Europe
5	Wohnort	E	Double room
6	die Vereinigten Staaten	F	Ticket
7	Europa	G	Wash-basin
8	mit zehn Minuten Verspätung	H	Restaurant car
9	Fahrkarte	I	Place of residence
10	Speisewagen	J	First name

38 Warning to Hotel Guests

Wir wollen Sie darauf aufmerksam machen, daß unser Hotel keinerlei Verantwortung für Verluste von Wertgegenständen, die nicht im Hotelsafe aufbewahrt werden, übernehmen.
Fragen Sie bitte für weitere Informationen im Büro nach (Parterre, Zimmer zwei) zwischen 12.00 und 14.00 oder zwischen 19.00 und 21.00.
Danke.

1 Where should valuables be left?
2 Where is the office where further information may be obtained?
3 How many hours a day is the office open to hotel guests?

39 Air Crash

Alle vierunddreissig Insassen sind gestern beim Absturz eines französischen Militärflugzeugs in der Nähe der südfranzösischen Stadt Béziers ums Leben gekommen.

Die Maschine prallte gegen einen Berg und explodierte.

1 How many people were travelling in the aircraft?
2 To which country did the aircraft belong?
3 In which part of the country is the town of Béziers?
4 What did the aircraft fly into, and what happened as a result of this?

40 Extract from a Guide-book

Dieses Schloß vor Ihnen wurde im vierzehnten Jahrhundert erbaut. Es besteht aus hundertfünfundzwanzig Räumen. Heutzutage wird es als Museum benutzt. Touristen aus ganz Europa kommen, um die historischen Kostüme, Gemälde und Möbel, die hier aufbewahrt werden, zu besichtigen. Das Schloß ist täglich zur Besichtigung geöffnet, ausser an Feiertagen. In den nächsten fünf Jahren sollen vierhunderttausend D-Mark in dieses Gebäude zur Renovierung investiert werden.

1 When was the castle built?
2 How many rooms does the castle comprise?
3 What use is made of the castle today?
4 Which *three* things do tourists come to see?
5 How much money is going to be spent on the castle, and when?

41 Stormy Weather

Schwere Stürme ereigneten sich gestern in Westdeutschland. Einige Dörfer in Bayern sind sogar ohne Elektrizität und Telephon. In Hessen besteht die Gefahr, daß einige Dörfer von der Außenwelt total abgeschnitten werden, wenn der Wasserspiegel weiterhin steigt. Die Einwohner bereiten sich vor, im Notfall ihre Häuser zu verlassen.

1 What have some Bavarian villages been deprived of?
2 Explain the danger threatening villages in Hessen.
3 What are the inhabitants preparing to do?

Assignment
(a) Use an atlas to locate the West German Länder (states) of Bavaria and Hessen.
(b) Of how many states does West Germany consist?
(c) Which is the largest West German state?
(d) Which is the most northerly West German state?

42 Leisure Time in West Germany

Here is an extract from a survey which tried to find out how West Germans spend their leisure time.

A: **Wenigstens dreimal pro Woche**	
Ich lese die Zeitung	76%
Ich lese Bücher	42%
Ich sehe fern	83%
Ich sitze im Garten/Park	13%
Ich höre Radio	52%
B: **Wenigstens einmal pro Woche**	
Ich stricke/nähe	71% (der Frauen)
Ich höre Schallplatten	59%
Ich plaudere mit Freunden/Freundinnen	49%
Ich lese Zeitschriften	47%
Ich schreibe Briefe	52%
Ich arbeite im Garten	42%
Ich spiele Karten	18%
Ich gehe ins Café/Lokal	74%
Ich treibe Sport	27%
Ich spiele Schach/Dame	8%
Ich spiele ein Instrument	3%
C: **Wenigstens einmal pro Monat**	
Ich besuche Freunde/Verwandte	65%
Ich mache Spaziergänge auf dem Lande	38%
Ich gehe ins Kino	30%
Ich gehe tanzen	17%
Ich gehe schwimmen	20%
Ich wasche das Auto	32%
Ich kaufe neue Kleider	61%
Ich gehe ins Restaurant	46%
D: **Wenigstens sechsmal pro Jahr**	
Ich gehe ins Konzert	24%
Ich gehe ins Museum	19%
Ich fahre ins Ausland	6%

Study the following statements about the survey and then decide which are true and which are false. Copy down those statements which you think are true.

1 Newspapers are read more often than books.
2 Radio is less popular than television.
3 Less than half the women interviewed knit once a week.
4 Playing chess or draughts is less popular than a game of cards.
5 Dancing is more popular than swimming.
6 59% of Germans listen to records at least once a day.
7 27% of Germans watch sport once a week.
8 Chatting with friends is less popular than going to a café or public house.
9 61% of Germans buy new clothes at least twelve times a year.
10 Playing a musical instrument is much less popular than chatting with friends.

Revision Test J

Give the meaning of these words and phrases chosen from exercises 38-42.

(a) Parterre
(b) Absturz
(c) Schloß
(d) Gemälde
(e) Möbel
(f) gestern
(g) Einwohner
(h) Schallplatten
(i) auf dem Lande
(j) Zeitschriften

43 A Ship Explodes

Gestern ereignete sich eine Explosion an Bord des westdeutschen Tankers *Klavigo*, der in Rotterdam mit einer Ladung von hundertfünfunddreißig Tonnen Öl vor Anker liegt.

Drei Seeleute wurden ins Krankenhaus gebracht. Feuerwehrleute kämpfen noch immer gegen die Flammen. Der Schaden wird hunderttausend D-Mark ausmachen.

1 What is the nationality of the ship?
2 Where is the vessel anchored?
3 What was the vessel's cargo?
4 What happened to the ship?
5 How many sailors were taken to hospital?
6 How much damage has been caused?

Assignment
(a) In which country is the city of Rotterdam?
(b) What is the importance of Rotterdam for the Ruhr industrial area of West Germany?

44 Two Road Accidents

A Gestern abend waren zwei junge Autofahrer bei einem Verkehrsunfall an der Straßenkreuzung Klemensstraße — Langenstraße in Minden verletzt. Der Fahrer eines blauen Volkswagens, der die Langenstraße entlangfuhr, stieß mit einem Opel zusammen. Der Fahrer des Opels, Anton Klein, 25, überfuhr eine rote Ampel und dann stieß in die rechte Hintertür des Volkswagens, dessen Fahrer zu spät bremste. Beide Straßen wurden von der Polizei gesperrt.

A 1 How many vehicles were involved in this first accident?
2 Who was responsible for the accident and in what way?
3 Which part of the Volkswagen was damaged?
4 What did the driver of the Volkswagen do to try to avoid a collision?
5 What did the police do after the accident?

B Gestern früh wurden auf der Autobahn in der Nähe von Ulm vier Menschen bei einem Verkehrsunfall schwer verletzt. Achtunddreißig Autos und zwei Schwertransporter waren betroffen. Wahrscheinlich wurde der Unfall von einem Autofahrer verursacht, der plötzlich bremste, als er in ein Nebelgebiet fuhr.

B 1 When did this second accident occur?
2 How many people were injured?
3 How many vehicles were involved in the accident altogether?
4 Explain how the accident is thought to have been caused.

45 At a Safari Park

Look at the advertisement opposite.

1 For how many hours a day is this safari park open in the Summer months, and at what time of year would it close earlier? Explain your answer.
2 How many animals can be found in this safari park, and from where do they come?
3 Name as many different animals in the safari park as you can.
4 Which of the following does the safari-park *not* mention in this notice?
(a) a chair-lift, (b) a miniature railway, (c) a boating lake, (d) a chimpanzees' tea-party, (e) dolphins, (f) wild deer.
5 What indicates that the park is in an attractive setting?
6 What signpost would you look for if approaching the safari park by motorway?

Safari-Tierpark

Täglich von 10 Uhr bis 1 Stunde vor Sonnenuntergang, längstens bis 18 Uhr, geöffnet

Löwen — Tiger — Wildschweine — Kamele — Großvögel — Affen — Elefanten — Bären: insgesamt über 500 Tiere aller Kontinente

Pony-Reiten — Spielplatz — Aquarium —
Kindereisenbahn —
Café-Restaurant —
Minigolf —
Automuseum — Sessellift —
Delphin-Show

MIT WEITEM BLICK AUF DAS RHEINTAL

Direkt an der Autobahn
(Ausfahrt Neustadt-Süd)
Gute Parkmöglichkeiten

Revision Test K

Give the meanings of these words chosen from exercises 43-45.

(a) Öl
(b) Seeleute
(c) Feuerwehrleute
(d) Schaden
(e) Verkehrsunfall
(f) Ampel
(g) Schwertransporter
(h) Autofahrer
(i) Sonnenuntergang
(j) Sessellift

46 Weather Forecast (3)

Wetter

Freitag, 15. Juni

Zone 1: Heiter bis wolkig, Höchsttemperatur 20 Grad. Morgen: Etwas wärmer.

Zone 2: Wolken und Sonne, Höchsttemperatur 17 bis 20 Grad. Morgen: Es wird wärmer.

Zone 3: Wolken, dabei freundlich, Höchsttemperatur 18 bis 20 Grad. Morgen: Wie heute.

Zone 4: Wolken und Sonne, Höchsttemperatur 18 bis 20 Grad. Morgen Weiterer Temperaturanstieg.

Zone 5: Sonnig und trokken. Höchsttemperatur um 22 Grad. Morgen: Beständig und warm.

Zone 6: Heiter bis wolkig, Höchsttemperatur 20 bis 23 Grad. Morgen: Das Wetter bleibt.

Zone 7: Wolken, dabei freundlich, Höchsttemperatur 20 bis 23 Grad. Morgen: Etwas wärmer.

Zone 8: Wolken und Sonne, Höchsttemperatur um 15 Grad. Morgen: Beständig.

Zone 9: Heiter bis wolkig, Höchsttemperatur 20 bis 24 Grad. Morgen: Wenig Änderung.

Zone 10: Wolken und Sonne, Höchsttemperatur um 20 Grad. Morgen: Freundlich.

1 For which day of the week is this weather forecast issued?
2 Which zone is expected to have the lowest temperature?
3 Which zones should have the same weather tomorrow as they will have today?
4 Which zones will have sunshine today?
5 Which zones will have warmer weather tomorrow?

47 A Shop is Burgled

Der Inhaber einer Blumenhandlung in der Moltkestraße kehrte gestern abend um 21.00 Uhr von einem Kinobesuch nach Hause zurück, als er ein Licht in dem Kellergeschoß seines Geschäfts bemerkte. Plötzlich stürzten drei maskierte Männer heraus und stiegen in ein gelbes Auto, das vor dem Geschäft wartete. Später entdeckte der Inhaber der Blumenhandlung, Ernst Kröger, 43, daß die Räuber vierhundert DM gestohlen hatten. Drei Männer wurden zwei Stunden später in einem Hamburger Restaurant von der Polizei verhaftet.

1 What kind of shop was burgled?
2 Where had the owner of the shop spent the evening?
3 How did the shop-owner first become aware that something was wrong?
4 How many men raced out of the shop?
5 Why would they have been difficult to identify?
6 What was waiting outside the shop?
7 How much money was stolen?
8 At what time of night were the thieves arrested?

48 A Strange Case For the Police

Seit dem Wochenende sucht die dänische Polizei eine fünfundzwanzigjährige Frau, die auf dem Fahrschiff zwischen Gedser und Travemünde verschwunden ist. Sie war mit zwei Familienangehörigen auf einem Ausflug nach Deutschland. Aus den Ermittlungen schließt die Polizei, daß sie nicht von Bord gefallen oder gesprungen sein kann. Die Polizei glaubt deshalb an eine Entführung. Die Dänin kann in einem Auto versteckt worden sein, das dann in Travemünde von Bord gefahren ist. Die blonde Dänin lebt in Belgien mit ihrem Mann, einem Profi-Fußballspieler.

1 This news report is about
(a) a young Danish boy who has disappeared
(b) a missing German woman in her twenties
(c) a young woman who may have been kidnapped
(d) a girl who has vanished on her way to Denmark
2 The missing person was travelling
(a) alone
(b) with two friends of the family
(c) in a large party
(d) with members of his or her family
3 Police have decided that the missing person
(a) was pushed into the sea
(b) may have leaped overboard
(c) must have driven off the boat in Denmark
(d) was hidden in a car
4 The police know that the missing person
(a) is a Danish footballer
(b) has fair hair and lives in Belgium
(c) is a professional sportsman
(d) is married to a Belgian

Revision Test L

Give the meanings of these words and phrases chosen from exercises 46-48.

(a) Höchsttemperatur
(b) zwanzig Grad
(c) freundlich
(d) die Blumenhandlung
(e) das Kellergeschoß
(f) verhaftet
(g) ein Fußballspieler
(h) eine Entführung

Final Test

These words and phrases have been chosen from exercises throughout the book. How many can you remember?

1 Regen
2 Kirche
3 Bahnhof
4 bitte
5 Gute Reise!
6 ein Pfund Zucker
7 dreißig Liter Benzin
8 Blick auf die See
9 Obsttorte
10 zwei Kilo Rosenkohl
11 Parken verboten
12 Bäckerei
13 Metzgerei
14 einmal zweiter Klasse nach Stuttgart
15 Kaffee mit Schlagsahne
16 Obstsalat
17 Rotwein
18 Nicht hinauslehnen
19 ein Kilo Erbsen
20 Eier
21 Sportnachrichten
22 rechts halten
23 nur für Radfahrer
24 Zoll
25 gehen Sie bei der Ampel rechts
26 Polizeiwache
27 reserviert
28 Kleider
29 Sonderangebote
30 Direktflug
31 Reisebüro
32 Staubsauger
33 zu Spottpreisen
34 U-Bahnhaltestelle
35 Winterschlußverkauf
36 Endspiel
37 Herren
38 Trinkwasser
39 im dritten Stock
40 gestohlen
41 Autonummer
42 ein kleines Zimmer mit zwei Betten
43 inklusiv Bedienung
44 Familienname
45 Süssigkeiten
46 Gleis fünf
47 Schalter drei
48 im vierzehnten Jahrhundert
49 drei Seeleute
50 Verkehrsunfall